Printed in the USA

The Lives of 33 Great Christians

BY JOHN STEIN

Contents

Introduction

World history is full of exciting and colorful events that surround the faithful believers of Jesus Christ. As Christians, it is important to study the history of our ancestors; their lives are a big part of our Christian heritage. World history is full of Christians who have shaped our world as well as their own lives through their faith in Jesus Christ. There have been many Christians throughout history that have relied on their faith in their everyday lives, as well as their professional and political lives.

While studying the history of Christians, you begin to realize how multinational and multiethnic the body of Christ actually is. This book explores some of these diverse people and how their beliefs made a difference in our world. We will be reminded of people who may be very familiar to most, such as George Washington, Ludwig van Beethoven, Mother Teresa, and Martin Luther King Jr. We will discuss the lives of those who you may have heard of, but may not have known were Christians, such as Christopher Columbus, Michelangelo, and Galileo Galilei. We will explore the lives of some lesser-known Christians such as, Ulrich Zwingli, Tertullian, and Cyril of Alexandria. Some of the people we will discuss are from fields we often associate with secular worldviews, such as scientists, politicians, and artists. Some were men and women who dedicated their careers to Christ, such as missionaries, preachers, and authors.

This book will explore the good times and difficult times in the lives of these Christians. The reader will see that it isn't always easy being a Christian. This book is full of people who, because of their faith, overcame obstacles and tragedy. Sometimes, these Christians knew the cost of their faith and other times, they were caught by surprise. Some of these men and women gave their lives for the One who promised he had overcome the world.

The common theme of each of their stories is one of faith and hope that the eternal rewards outweigh the struggles and battles of this world.

These lives are our Christian heritage and should be remembered for their contribution to this world. This is certainly not an exclusive list and there are countless others who have stories just as powerful, just as important as these are.

Martin Luther (1483 – 1546)

You shall not follow a crowd to do evil; nor shall you testify in a dispute so as to turn aside after many to pervert justice. Exodus 23:2

Martin Luther was a Christian theologian and Augustinian monk. His teachings inspired the Protestant Reformation. His life marks a major turning point in western history, as well as Christianity itself.

Martin was born in Eisleben, Germany to Margaret and Hans Luder. He was raised in Mansfeld, where his father worked at the local copper mines. Martin attended Latin school and by the age of thirteen, he studied law at the University of Erfurt, where he received his bachelor's, and master's degrees. He earned the nickname "The Philosopher" because of his strong skills at public debates. He eventually earned his doctorate in the Bible and became a professor at Wittenberg University.

In 1505, at 21 years of age, Luther was nearly struck by lightning. He then vowed to become a monk if he were saved. He gave away all of his possessions and became a monk. He did well and took his life as a monk seriously; he excelled at praying, fasting, as well as other ascetic practices. While at Wittenberg University, he began to question some of the ways and teachings of the church.

In 1517, on All Saints Eve, Luther posted a notice on the door of the Wittenberg Church that listed 95 theses that he wanted to debate. This list of theses quickly spread across Germany as a call to reform the church. Without really meaning to, Luther questioned the authority of the church and brought about the Protestant Reformation. Luther was threatened with excommunication because of his questioning, but was hidden in a castle in Saxony. He spent his time translating the Bible into German.

Luther insisted that the Bible alone should be the standard by which Christians live their lives, not by doing works as directed by the church. Luther argued three points. 1) That all Christians were priests. He encouraged rulers to take up the cause of the reform. 2) He reduced the seven sacraments down to two—baptism and the Lord's Supper. 3) He told Christians they were free from the law, but bound in love to their neighbors.

Luther's rebellion against the church accomplished many things that moved many Christians in a direction that was pleasing to God. Luther insisted that people should have the Bible written in their own language. He began and led the way for reform in the church and inspired many reformers to come after him. His reform ushered the world out of the Middle Ages and into the modern era. By 1546, the year of his death, much of northern Europe had become Protestant.

Augustine of Hippo (354 – 430)

Preach the word! Be ready in season and out of season. Convince, rebuke, exhort, with all longsuffering and teaching. 2 Timothy 4:2

Augustine was a bishop, philosopher, and theologian who spent much of his life seeking the truth and peace of God. Most scholars agree that he was the most important figure in the ancient Western church.

Augustine was born in Tagaste, Numidia in Northern Africa to a pagan father and a Christian mother. His childhood was pretty unremarkable. He studied rhetoric at Carthage. Despite his mother's attempts at raising him as a Christian, Augustine was captivated by pagan philosophers. He drifted through many philosophical belief systems before he converted to Christianity in his early 30s. For a time, he was a Manichean, a religion that contradicted Christianity. While teaching in Italy, he was influenced by Bishop Ambrose and he was baptized in 387. He found the only true philosophy and source of righteous living in Christianity.

He developed his own approach to philosophy and theology; helping to formulate the doctrine known as original sin. His thoughts had a profound influence on the medieval worldview. We know him as Augustine of Hippo because the citizens of the northern Africa city insisted that he be their bishop. While in Hippo, Augustine wrote about many of the religious controversy of his time. He wrote against Manichaeism, his former religion. He also wrote against Pelagianism, a Christian heresy that taught people they could save themselves through their own efforts.

Augustine was one of the most prolific Latin authors, with more than 100 separate titles; including apologetic and exegetical works, as well as many letters and sermons. He is best known for his autobiographical work called *Confessions, which* consists of 13 books that give a personal account of his early life. His writings were very influential in the development of Western Christianity.

He was a relentless truth-seeker who eventually found God. Augustine left behind many writings that still fascinate and influence theologians of today.

Billy Graham (1918 -   )

But you shall receive power when the Holy Spirit has come upon you; and you shall be witnesses to Me in Jerusalem, and in all Judea and Samaria, and to the end of the earth. Acts 1:8

Billy Graham was a revival, television, and radio evangelist. He has been called the "Pope of Protestant America. He is best known for his evangelistic crusades in which he preached the Gospel to more people that anyone else in history.

William Franklin Graham Jr. was born in Charlotte, NC in 1918 where he was raised on a dairy farm. He dreamed of becoming a professional baseball player. He was educated at Bob Jones College, Florida Bible Institute, and Wheaton College.

When Graham was 16 years old, he was moved by a series of revival meetings being held by evangelist Mordecai Ham. He was ordained by the Southern Baptist Convention in 1939. He began his career as a pastor, soon joining a missionary group called Youth for Christ. On June 1, 1957, the first live television broadcast of a Graham crusade reached about 6.4 million viewers.

Graham has served as a United States presidential advisor for Eisenhower, Johnson, and Nixon. He also authored more than 30 books, many of which were printed in several languages. Some of his works included, The Reason for Hope: Salvation, The Journey, The Jesus Generation and more.

Graham's integrity and charismatic approach to preaching the Gospel has been an encouragement for millions, including Martin Luther King, Jr. and many of the United States presidents from Eisenhower to Bush. He has preached the Gospel live to an estimated 215 million people in over 185 countries and millions more have heard him through television, radio, and film.

Graham has received many awards and honors for his preaching over the years, including the Ronald Reagan Presidential Foundation Freedom Award, The Congressional Gold Medal, etc.

C.S. Lewis (1898 – 1963)

Then you will understand the fear of the Lord, and find the knowledge of God. Proverbs 2:5

C.S. Lewis was an Irish author and scholar who was best known for his fantasy series called Chronicles of Narnia. He wrote about 40 books. He was a professor and Christian apologist.

Clive Staples Lewis was born in Belfast, Ireland in 1898. As a child, he was fascinated by animals and tales of gallantry. He was reading by three years old and began writing fairytales at age five. Reading and education were very important to his parents. He was educated at home until he was enrolled in boarding school at 10 years old, after his mother died. He studied literature and philosophy at Oxford University. Lewis was a professor of literature at Oxford and Cambridge.

Lewis' conversion came as much of a surprise to him as those around him. He was an atheist who slowly realized that God was after his heart. Lewis was interested in and challenged by the writings of Christian authors George MacDonald and G.K. Chesterton. Many of his friends were Christians as well, including author J.R.R. Tolkien. Lewis eventually converted and joined the Church of England because of the influence of these men. In his own words: "God has not been trying to experiment on my faith or love in order to find out their quality. He knew it already. It was I who didn't. In this trial, He makes us occupy the dock, the witness box, and the bench all at once. He always knew that my temple was a house of cards. His only way of making me realize the fact was to knock it down."

Lewis life changed immediately as did the direction of his writing. *The Pilgrim's Progress: An Allegorical Apology for Christianity, Reason, and Romanticism* was published within two years of his conversion. As an apologetic writer, Lewis used logic and philosophy to support his Christian faith. He published 25 Christian books, including the classics *Mere Christianity, The Screwtape Letters, The Chronicles of Narnia,*

Miracles, The Four Loves, and Surprised by Joy, which was an autobiographical account of his conversion. Even in his fiction works, he incorporated Christian themes and symbols throughout.

In spite of his great success as an author, Lewis remained humble. Instead of increasing his standard of living, he increased his support for charity. He had a gift for words and many of his quotes are still used by Christians. His works remain popular with Christians and non-Christians alike.

Christopher Columbus (1450 – 1506)

Those who go down to the sea in ships, who do business on great waters, they see the works of the Lord, and His wonders of the deep. Psalm 107:23-24

Christopher Columbus was an Italian explorer, navigator, and colonizer that discovered the "New World" of the Americas. Many believed he was responsible for bringing the Christian faith to "half the world".

Christopher was born in 1451 in the Republic of Genoa, Italy. He was a devout Catholic who prayed regularly and observed the fasts of the church.

Columbus had the "crazy" idea that he could reach India by sailing west so that trade with Asia would be easier. At the time, European traders either made the dangerous voyage around the tip of Africa or they travelled across the land through hostile territory. Many people thought Columbus was crazy; however, he was not going into this voyage blindly. He estimated the size of the Atlantic Ocean by reading his Bible. If he succeeded in finding a western trade route to India, it would not only increase trade, but would also open up a new mission field for Christians. Queen Isabella of Spain was so impressed by Columbus that she agreed to back his voyage.

Columbus' first voyage west was long and difficult, many of his men wanted to give up, they even threatened mutiny. However, Columbus believed that God wanted him to keep sailing, so he did. He finally reached what was the Bahamas off the coast of Florida, convinced that he had reached Asia. He named the island San Salvador meaning, "Holy Savior". After sighting land, Columbus prayed, "O Lord, Almighty and everlasting God, by Thy holy Word Thou hast created the heaven, and the earth, and the sea; blessed and glorified by Thy Name, and praised be Thy Majesty, which hath designed to use us, Thy humble servants, that Thy Names may be proclaimed in this second part of the earth."

Columbus was a determined and courageous man who took his faith seriously. He understood the importance of delivering the message of the gospel. Unlike many sailors, he did not use profanity. He also observed religious rites on his voyages.

Unfortunately, many of the Spanish settlers treated the Native Americans shamefully; however, Columbus' voyages did lead to the evangelizing of two continents. During the years 1493 – 1820, Spain sent over 15,000 missionaries to the Americas and it is believed that during the first fifteen years after Columbus' discovery that over 5 million Native Americans were baptized.

Helen Keller (1880 - 1968)

But those who wait on the Lord shall renew their strength; they shall mount up with wings like eagles, they shall run and not be weary, they shall walk and not faint. Isaiah 40:31

Helen Keller was an American author, speaker, and political activist. She was deaf and blind, but that did not stop her from becoming world famous.

Helen Adams Keller was born in Tuscumbia, Alabama in 1880. She was born with the ability to see and hear; however, at 19 months old she contracted a disease that left her blind and deaf.

Keller's mother, inspired by a blind and deaf woman in Charles Dickens' *American Notes*, began a search to find a way to educate Keller when she was seven years old. This exhaustive search led her to Anne Sullivan who became Keller's teacher, governess, and then eventually her friend.

Keller attended the Perkins Institute for the Blind, the Wright-Humanson School for the Deaf, the Cambridge School for Young Ladies, and finally Radcliffe College where she became the first blind and deaf person to earn a Bachelor of Arts degree at the age of 24. Keller was able to "read" people's lips by touch. She was also proficient at using Braille and sign language. She was determined to communicate with others as conventionally as possible, so she learned to speak. In fact, she spent her life giving speeches and lectures. As an author, she had twelve published books as well as many more articles.

She was an advocate for people with disabilities. She is the co-founder of Helen Keller International, an organization that is devoted to research in vision, health, and nutrition. She also helped found the American Civil Liberties Union.

She was awarded the Presidential Medal of Freedom in 1964 and elected into the National Women's Hall of fame in 1965. Keller's story of triumph over her disabilities is one of the most inspiring stories of our time and offers hope to many. Her ability to live fully, in spite of her physical challenges, is a great testament to her faith.

Cyril of Alexandria (376 – 444)

Now then, we are ambassadors for Christ, as though God were pleading through us; we implore you on Christ's behalf, be reconciled to God. 2 Corinthians 5:20

Cyril of Alexandria was the Christian patriarch of Alexandria. He was a scholarly archbishop and a prolific writer. He served as Pope of Alexandria from 412 – 444.

Cyril was born in Theodosios, Egypt. Cyril was well educated because of his uncle's position of patriarch of Alexandria. Cyril became pope after the death of his uncle, at a time when Alexandria was at the height in influence and power within the Roman Empire. He used his position of power within the Roman Empire to champion the orthodox faith. He was named a doctor of the church in 1882.

Cyril was considered a political and religious leader in Egypt. He was active in the complex doctrinal struggles of the 5th century, which focused on the nature of the personhood of Christ. He is widely known for his campaign against Nestorius, the bishop of Constantinople. Cyril argued for the single divine subjectivity of Christ, describing how it encompasses a full and authentic humanity in Jesus.

Cyril wrote extensively and was a leading protagonist in the controversies of his time. He also wrote many exegeses, including *Commentaries on the Old Testament, Thesaurus, Discourse Against Arians, Commentary on St. John's Gospel, and Dialogues on the Trinity.*

His writings and theology remain an important part of the tradition of the Church Fathers today. His supporters call him a "Pillar of Faith" and "Seal of the Fathers".

Dwight L. Moody (1837 – 1899)

Declare His glory among the nations, His wonders among all peoples. 1 Chronicles 16:23

Dwight L. Moody (D.L. Moody) was an American evangelist and publisher. He founded the Moody Church, Northfield, and Mount Herman Schools in Massachusetts, the Moody Bible Institute, and Moody Publishers.

Moody was born in Northfield, Massachusetts in 1837. His father died when Moody was just four, leaving his mother to raise nine children. His family was very poor, his mother never encouraged Bible study, and he only received the equivalent of a fifth-grade education.

At 17, Moody moved to Boston to work as a shoe salesman in his uncle's shoe store. His uncle required him to attend church. He was attending Sunday School classes and because of the kindness of his teacher, he became a Christian at 18 years old. He immediately began sharing his faith with others.

He originally set out to make a fortune, but his newfound faith caused him to change his focus. He decided to focus his life on feeding the poor. He became involved in the US Christian Commission of the YMCA. Moody once said, "There are many of us that are willing to o great things for the Lord, but few of us are willing to do little things."

Moody conducted revivals and directed Bible conferences where he preached "the old-fashioned gospel." Moody's revivals were financed by businessmen who believed he could help the poor.

He preached throughout the United States and Great Britain, emphasizing a literal interpretation of the Bible. He was also present among the Union soldiers during the Civil War and was always on the mission field regardless of where he was.

D.L. Moody didn't attend school past the fifth grade; he couldn't spell and his grammar was terrible. His manners were sometimes crude and he never became an ordained minister. God used this broken man to lead thousands, probably more, of people to confess their faith in Christ.

Galileo Galilei (1564 – 1642)

And they will turn their ears away from the truth, and be turned aside to fables. 2 Timothy 4:4

Galileo Galilei was an Italian physicist, mathematician, astronomer, and philosopher of the 17th century. He was famous for his scientific achievements in astronomy, mathematics, and physics. He pioneered observations that laid the foundation for modern physics and astronomy, as well as improved the telescope. He was also known as "The Father of Modern Science".

Galileo was born in Pisa in the Duchy of Florence, Italy. He studied medicine at the University of Pisa, but dropped out of school and never got a university degree. He then studied on his own, and became a tutor.

Galileo believed in observing nature in controlled conditions and providing mathematical results. This resulted in discourse between Galileo and the "natural philosophers" at the University of Pisa where he was the chair of mathematics. They came to their scientific conclusions by arguing the works of Aristotle. This was in contrast to Galileo's method of study. Galileo publically humiliated them, which only made their relations worse. After only two years at Pisa, he left and spent the next 18 years at the University of Padua. This was a more progressive institution, allowing Galileo to explore physics in his own way.

He was a devout Christian who saw a marriage between science and religion. He said, "God is known by nature in his works, and by doctrine in his revealed word." Galileo believed that proper interpretation of the Bible would agree with observed fact.

In a letter to the Grand Duchess of Tuscany, Galileo expressed his scientific views that supported Copernicus. This letter was in conflict with the Church's Aristotelian science tradition and thus resulted in his conviction on suspicion of heresy, which led to a lifetime of house arrest.

The Church eventually could not deny the truth that Galileo taught and in 1758, lifted the ban on his works.

While many view Galileo's conflict with the Church as a victory over religion, Galileo would disagree. His faith in the truth of god's Word remained strong, even in the end. He recognized God as King and Creator.

George W. Bush (1946 -   )

Watch, stand fast in faith, be brave, be strong. 1 Corinthians 16:13

George W. Bush was a businessman, governor, and the 43rd President of the United States. He is known for leading the United States in response to the terrorist attacks in 2001.

George Walker Bush was born in New Haven, Connecticut in 1946. His father was the 41st president of the United States. His family moved to Texas, where he grew up. He was educated at Yale University and Harvard Business School. He enlisted in the Texas Air National Guard in 1968, at the height of the Vietnam War. He made his living in the oil business in Texas.

In 1986, Bush overcame alcoholism when he converted to Christianity. He turned to the Bible to save his marriage and family. Bush's spiritual beliefs shaped his private life as well as his public policies and politics. He has been very open about the role of faith in his life. He has often said that faith saved his life, nurtured his family, and established his political career. "My faith plays a big part in my life…I pray for strength. I pray for wisdom. I pray for troops in harm's way. I pray for my family."

His presidency was faith-based. He often uses Scripture during his speeches, relying on his faith to direct his actions. He brought his deep religious beliefs to his job. He appointed other, like-minded Christians to political office. He supported faith-based initiatives and swore to keep "under God" in the *Pledge of Allegiance.* He used his faith to guide him during the tragedy of the September 11th terrorist attacks and this faith enabled him to lead a grieving nation as well.

Bush's faith sets him apart from others who have held his position. It defines him as a man, a husband, a father, and his role in the political world. There are many events and people in his life that led his to a life of Christianity, but it is clear that these beliefs and strong faith have been rock solid since his conversion. He serves as inspiration for Christian politicians in today's highly secular political world.

George Washington (1731 – 1799)

Blessed is the nation whose God is the Lord, the people He has chosen as His own inheritance. Psalms 33:12

George Washington was one of the Founding Fathers of the United States, the leader of the Continental Army during the American Revolution and the first president of the United States.

Washington was born in Westmoreland County, Virginia in 1732. His Great-Grandfather migrated from England, making Washington the third generation of his family to be born in America. His family was members of the "middling class" in Virginia. While there are many fables about it, not much is known about his early childhood. Washington was homeschooled and learned from the local church sexton and eventually a schoolmaster.

Washington served as a general and commander –in-chief of the colonial armies during the American Revolution. Accepted by a majority of Americans, he served as the first President of the United States from 1789 to 1797. He received pressure to serve a third term; however, he felt the decline of his physical health and refused. In his Farewell Address to the Nation, he addressed the nation one last time before the end of his presidency urging the people to cherish the Union and avoid partisanship and permanent foreign alliances. Many of the forms of government he established are still being used today.

Although there is some question regarding the faith of Washington it is believed that he was an Episcopalian. He did not openly write about his religious beliefs, but he did practice his religion while he was president— regularly attending church services. He was an early supporter of religious freedom and believed that all religions were beneficial.

Washington could have been a king, but he chose to be a citizen. His actions in Office set many precedents for the United States government. He was a man of integrity with a deep sense of duty, honor, and patriotism. There are many monuments, memorials, libraries, schools, etc. all over the country in memory and honoring his service to America. His face is on the one-dollar bill, as well as the front of the quarter. His legacy is one of the greatest in American history.

Hernan Cortes (1485 – 1547)

I have pursued my enemies and overtaken them; neither did I turn back again till they were destroyed. Psalm 18:37

Hernan Cortes was a Spanish conquistador and explorer who overthrew the Aztec empire and claimed Mexico for Spain. He was one of Spain's most influential conquistadors and played an important role in the advancement of Spain's power in North America in the 1500s.

Hernando Cortes, marques del Valle de Oaxaca was born in 1485 in Medellin, Spain. Not much is known about his childhood, but he is believed to have studied law at the University of Salamanca, but that didn't last long because he was an explorer at heart and in 1504, he left to seek his fortune in the New World.

He was only 19 years old when he first voyaged to the New World, where he settled in Santo Domingo. While there, he joined other expeditions; however, in 1518, he commanded his own expedition to Mexico. Cortes reached the Mexican coast in 1519 with 650 men. He fought with some of the natives, but made many alliances. He used these alliances with the local Indian tribes to help him conquer the Aztecs, a fierce and cruel people who ruled the tribes around them, using them as human sacrifices. Cortes wanted to overthrow the Aztecs to claim the land and gold they possessed for Spain. He succeeded in his conquest when he took control of the Aztec empire in 1521. He became the governor of "New Spain". He was eventually removed from the throne and spent his final years in Spain.

Although some criticize because Cortes was a powerful Spanish conqueror and at times ordered the violent death of his enemies, he was a Christian. He urged the Indian chiefs to forsake their idols and replace them with a Christian alter. When he came upon a room filled with Aztec idols, he said, "O God, why do you permit the Devil to be so greatly honored in this land?" He was clearly disturbed by the site. Regardless of what you believe of his intentions, you cannot dispute that he had a positive effect on the Indians he helped convert to Christianity.

Margaret Thatcher (1925 – 2013)

Behold, how good and how pleasant it is for brethren to dwell together in unity! Psalm 133:1

Margaret Thatcher was born Margaret Roberts in Grantham, Lincolnshire in 1925. She was raised as a Wesleyan Methodist. Her father, Alfred Roberts, was very active in church and politics; he was the mayor of Grantham. Margaret earned a scholarship to Kesteven and Grantham Girls' School where she was known for her hard work and determination. She attended Oxford University and received her Bachelor of Science degree. She married Denis Thatcher in 1951, thus becoming Margaret Thatcher.

Thatcher was the Prime Minister of the United Kingdom from 1979 to 1990. She dominated British and global politics in the 1980s. She was the only female Prime Minister of the UK and was the longest-serving British Prime Minister of the 20th Century. She rose to power during a time of great political and economic turmoil. Thatcher's political views were mostly based on her religious beliefs. She was considered a leader of Christian conviction and her uncompromising leadership style earned her the nickname, "Iron Lady".

After she was elected in 1979, Thatcher paraphrased the prayer *Make Me an Instrument of Your Peace* on the steps of 10 Downing Street. The words sum up her mission as a politician: "Where there is discord, may we bring harmony. Where there is error, may we bring truth. Where there is doubt, may we bring faith. And where there is despair, may we bring hope."

She was a leader of Christian conviction. In an article written for *The Daily Telegraph* in 1978, Thatcher wrote, "… the notion that we are all members one of another. It is expressed most vividly in the Christian concept of the Church as the Body of Christ; from this we learn the importance of interdependence and the truth that the individual achieves his own fulfillment only in service to others and to God." She made it clear that personal responsibility was important for a functioning society. Her matter-of-fact statements about Christianity and politics were seen as unusual for a politician.

In 2007, Thatcher became the first living British Prime Minister to be honored with a statue in the Houses of Parliament. After her death in 2013, there were mixed feelings from supporters and critics. Thatcher changed the nature of British society during her time in office. She will be remembered for her achievements in her life, as well as her example of having a strong belief in Christ and His Word. She was courageous in times of crisis and left a legacy that will inspire generations to come.

J. K. Rowling (1965 -   )

And He opened their understanding, that they might comprehend the Scriptures. Luke 24:45

J.K. Rowling is a British author and teacher who wrote the famous Harry Potter series.

Born Joanne Rowling in Yate, Gloucestershire, England in 1965. She grew up near Bristol, England. She wrote fantasy stories that she read to her sister. Her family was Anglican, but she later converted to the Church of Scotland. She attended Wyedean School and College and later graduated from Exeter University and became a teacher.

Rowling began writing the Harry Potter Series in 1990, which chronicled the life of a young wizard and his cohorts at the Hogwarts School of Witchcraft and Wizardry. Her Harry Potter book series made her a wildly popular author in the 1990s. In 1999, the first three books in the series were in the top three positions on *The New York Times* bestseller list, with over 35 million copies in print worldwide. It was available in 35 languages across the globe. The fourth book in the series, *Harry Potter and the Goblet of Fire,* was the fastest selling book of all time.

Although she has received criticism from Christians for the themes in her books, many believe the Harry Potter series is a Christian allegory. Rowling was silent on the topic until the release of her seventh book in the series. She admitted in an interview that her books were inspired by Christian themes. "To me [the religious parallels have] always been obvious," she said in an MTV interview on the topic. "But I never wanted to talk too openly about it because I thought it might show people, who just wanted the story, where we were going."

Her books have become the best-selling book series in history, having sold over 400 million copies. She has won multiple awards and inspired a series of films that became the highest-grossing film series of all time.

Although she is finished with the Harry Potter series, Rowling continues to write today and of course, reap the rewards of the success of the harry Potter series.

Saint Patrick (ca. 387 – 493)

Go into the all the world and preach the gospel to every creature. Mark 16:15

St. Patrick is Ireland's patron saint. He was a Romano-British missionary and Bishop in the 5th century. He is revered by Christians for establishing the church in Ireland. Known as the "Apostle of Ireland", the people of Ireland have observed St. Patrick's Day as a religious holiday for more than 1000 years.

Patrick was born in an English village called Bannavem Taberniae. Despite having a rich heritage in the Church, he was not raised in a religious home. He did not have much education as a boy and this would become a source of humiliation for him.

When Patrick was 16 years old, he was captured from his home by Irish pirates, brought to Ireland, and sold into slavery. While tending his master's sheep, he was called to Christ; in his own words, *"the Lord opened my mind to an awareness of my unbelief, in order that, even so late, I might remember my transgressions and turn with all my heart to the Lord my God, who had regard for my insignificance and pitied me in my youth and ignorance. He watched over me before I knew him, and before I had enough sense to distinguish between good and evil, and He protected me, and consoled me as a father would his son."* For the six years he was enslaved, he spent much of his time in prayer and had many visionary dreams. He was determined to convert the people of Ireland to Christianity and free them from the control of Druidism. Patrick eventually escaped his life as a slave and returned home to England.

Patrick went to France and worked to enter the priesthood under St. Germain. C. 431, St. Patrick Bishop of Ireland was consecrated by Pope St. Celestine. Since St. Patrick was still determined to convert the people of Ireland, he was sent to Ireland to spread the gospel. St. Patrick spread the news of Christianity quickly through preaching and writing. He won them over with the promise of becoming "the people of the Lord and the sons of God" and he baptized countless Irish people.

St. Patrick was successful in bringing the Gospel to Ireland. Christians honor him each year on the date of his death, March 17. St. Patrick was never canonized as a pope; however, he is on the list of Saints. He was venerated in the Orthodox Catholic Church.

J.R.R. Tolkien (1892 – 1973)

And all ends of the earth shall see the salvation of our God. Isaiah 52:10

J.R.R. Tolkien was an English writer, poet, philologist, and professor. He is best known for his works, The Hobbit and the Lord of the Rings Trilogy. His works have been made into award-winning films.

John Ronald Reuel Tolkien was born in Bloemfontein, South Africa in 1892. His father, Arthur Tolkien died when Tolkien was just four years old. He grew up with his mother and younger brother in Birmingham England. His mother home-schooled him and was an early reader, so she allowed him to read many books. He was especially interested in language, so she taught him Latin at a very young age. His mother died when Tolkien was twelve years old and was then under the care of a Catholic priest at the request of his mother, so the boys would be brought up as good Catholics. Tolkien went on to study at Exeter College and later taught at Oxford University.

Tolkien was a devout Roman Catholic. He was a traditionalist moderate, with libertarian and monarchist leanings. Theology and imagery played a role in Tolkien's creative imagination. Tolkien believed that his storytelling was a way to conceal Christian truth into the minds of secular readers. If you pay close attention, you will find glimpses of biblical truth in Tolkien's books. His works teach lessons in free will, making wise choices, and that it is possible to live a morally heroic life. Tolkien once said:

"The *Lord of the Rings* is of course a fundamentally religious and Catholic work; unconsciously so at first, but consciously in the revision. That is why I have not put in, or have cut out, practically all references to anything like 'religion', to cults or practices, in the imaginary world. For the religious element is absorbed into the story and the symbolism."

Tolkien was a close friend of C.S. Lewis; in fact, he played a significant role in the conversion of his friend from atheism to Christianity.

Tolkien's two most popular works, *The Hobbit* and the *Lord of the Rings,* have sold tens of millions of copies and are among the most popular books in the world. His works have reached many unsuspecting secularists with a Christian message and ideals.

Pope John Paul II (1920 – 2005)

I have fought the good fight, I have finished the race. I have kept the faith.
2 Timothy 4:7

Pope John Paul II was a Roman Catholic priest who eventually rose to become Pope. He was an advocate for human rights and is credited with the fall of communism in Poland.

John Paul II was born Karol Jozef Wojtyla in Wadowice, Poland in 1920. His childhood was filled with great loss; his mother and older brother died within a few years. He was an athletic young man and studied theater and poetry at Jagiellonian University. After the school was closed by Nazi's, John Paul began studying at a secret seminary in his pursuit to become a priest. After World War II ended, he completed his studies at a Krakow seminary and was ordained in 1946. He eventually got a doctorate in theology in Rome.

John Paul was one of the Catholic Church's leading thinkers of his time and made great contributions, therefore advancing in the Church. He became the bishop of Ombi in 1958, and the archbishop of Krakow in 1964. He was made a cardinal in 1967 and became pope in 1978, the first non-Italian pope in over 400 years.

John Paul was a charismatic man and was able to influence people to bring about political change. As an advocate for human rights, John Paul often spoke out about human suffering. He strongly opposed capital punishment. He travelled extensively in a successful attempt to improve relations with other faiths, including the Anglican Communion, Judaism, the Eastern Orthodox Church, and Islam.

In an attempted assassination, a Turk named Mehmet Ali Agca shot the Pope in 1981. He took four bullets total, two to the abdomen, causing profuse bleeding and a loss of three-fourths of his blood. After his miraculous recovery, having already forgiven him, he asked the people to pray for the gunman. He met privately with Agca to reconcile and show his forgiveness, a gesture that embodies the pope's character.

John Paul was well loved worldwide. When he died in 2005, more than 3 million people waited in line to say goodbye. In 2014, John Paul was made a saint.

John Calvin (1509 – 1564)

For you were once darkness, but now you are light in the Lord. Walk as children of light. Ephesians 5:8

John Calvin was an influential French author, pastor, and theologian during the time of the Protestant Reformation. He was Martin Luther's successor and was the key figure in the development of Christian theology, which would later become known as Calvinism.

John Calvin was born in Noyon, France in 1509. He studied law at the University of Orleans.

After converting to the Protestant religion, he settled in Geneva because France was hostile to Protestants. Calvin was at the forefront of church reform in Geneva. Because of his influence, and power, Geneva became home to many Protestants from all over Europe that were fleeing persecution. He established primary and secondary schools, as well as the University of Geneva to spread his teachings.

In his attempt to standardize the theories of Protestantism, Calvin published a masterpiece of theology called *Institutes of the Christian Religion* articulating his Protestant views. Calvin encouraged Christians to hold high moral standards. Calvin said that in order to know ourselves, we must know God. He often preached about the joy of being in a loving fellowship with God.

Some of the more prominent Calvinist supporters were John Knox, who brought Calvinism to Scotland and George Whitfield, one of the prominent leaders of the Methodist movement, who took Calvinism to the American colonies.

Calvin was an early riser and hard worker who always gave his best. His lifestyle of always pushing things to the limit may have led to his early death in 1564. He was a brilliant man who sparked a movement that revolutionized the Christian church throughout the world. Among his greatest accomplishments, were his writings, which were written for the purpose of leading men to love and enjoy God. While today's Christians do not agree with all of his teachings, such as *predestination*; many of his teachings are still practiced, such as *Once saved, always saved.* His writings have influenced Protestants for five centuries.

Winston Churchill (1874 – 1965)

Fear not, for I am with you; be not dismayed, for I am your God. I will strengthen you, Yes, I will help you, I will uphold you with My righteous right hand. Isaiah 41:10

Sir Winston Churchill was a British politician, Army officer, writer, and artist. He was Prime Minister of the United Kingdom from 1940 to 1945 and 1951 to 1955. He is regarded as one of the greatest wartime leaders of the twentieth century.

Winston Leonard Spencer-Churchill was born in Oxfordshire, England in 1874 to an aristocratic family. He grew up in Dublin, Ireland. He did not do well in school because he was a rebellious student. He ended up attending a boarding school near London called Harrow School. He eventually ended up attending and graduating from the British Royal Military College.

After graduation, Churchill joined the British Calvary. He had the opportunity to travel during his service. He then worked as a newspaper correspondent; he wrote stories about his military experience. He was captured in South Africa and became a Prisoner of War during the Second Boer War. He escaped from prison and travelled 300 miles to be rescued. This made him a hero in the eyes of his country. Over the next 30 years, he held many offices in Parliament.

When World War II began, the current Prime Minister did not see Adolf Hitler and the Germans as a treat to their country. Churchill warned the government and eventually was chosen as the prime Minister in 1940. Churchill inspired the Britains to keep fighting. He worked to forge an alliance with the United States and the Soviet Union. With the Allied Forces standing with them, they were able to fight off the Germans. Churchill's leadership helped Britain to stand against the Germans in World War II.

Regarding the faith of Churchill, he grew up in an Anglican household and referenced God during speeches, but there is no hard evidence of his beliefs or faith denomination. There is much debate about the faith of Churchill, but it is clear; however, that God used him to lead the Allied Forces to defeat Hitler in World War II.

Pocahontas/Rebecca Rolfe (1595 – 1617)

When a man's ways please the Lord, he makes even his enemies to be at peace with him. Psalm 16:7

Pocahontas, meaning "playful one", was a Native American princess who played an important role in the lives of the first colonists in Jamestown, Virginia. She became legendary when she stepped in to save John Smith's life. She was known by many other names throughout her life, as was common with Indians of that time, including Matoaka (her given name), Amounute, White Feather, and later Rebecca Rolfe (her Christian name). She is thought to be the first person to be converted to Christianity in America.

Pocahontas was born in Tsenacommacah (now known as Tidewater, Virginia) in 1595 to Powhatan, the chief of the Algonquian Indian tribes. She was sent with her mother as a young child, and then returned to live with her father as she began to mature. Like most young Indian girls, she learned how to forage for food, farming, and building houses.

Pocahontas' relationship with John Smith, an English colonist, was the reason she was linked so closely with the colonists in Jamestown. Smith was captured by an Indian and was brought to Chief Powhatan. Legend has it that she asked her father to spare his life, and he complied. After this, she often visited John Smith and helped the Jamestown colonists with survival skills. She kept them from starving to death that first winter. She stopped visiting Jamestown when she was told that her friend, John Smith, was dead. This was not true; he had only returned England for medical treatment. That ended up being a costly lie for the colonists because the following winter was known as the Starving Time. They did not see her for several years after that.

Pocahontas was captured by the English colonists in 1613 with the intentions of being traded for concessions from Powhatan. During this time, the colonists worked to convert her to Christianity. She and one of the colonists, John Rolfe, fell in love and she was baptized in 1614. She was given the name Rebecca Rolfe because of her conversion. The two married and created a time of peace between Jamestown and Powhatan's tribes called "Peace of Pocahontas".

Rebecca Rolfe visited England in 1616 where she was introduced to many important people, including King James and Queen Anne. As she was preparing to return home to the New World, she came down with an English disease that took her life. She was only 21 years old, but her impact on the New World during her short time was very important. When it comes to early American history, you may hear her called peacemaker, ambassador, even "Mother of the New World".

John Quincy Adams (1767 - 1848)

But you must continue in the things you have learned and been assured of, knowing from whom you have learned them. 2 Timothy 3:14

John Quincy Adams was the sixth president of the United States. Even more remarkable, however, is his spiritual life. He was one of America's greatest diplomats. He was known to many as "old Man Eloquent" for his support of freedom of speech.

Adams was born in Braintree, Massachusetts in 1767. His father was John Adams, the second president of the United States. He watched the battle of Bunker Hill in 1775, literally witnessing the birth of the United States. He often accompanied his father and other diplomats during the Revolution. He attended schools in Europe and then completed his education at Harvard, graduating in 1787.

Adams had a long career in public service, serving as ambassador to the Netherlands, Portugal, and Russia; senator; congressman; secretary of state; and of course, president of the United States. As president, he wanted to promote education and modernize the economy. He was also strongly against slavery. He was up against strong opposition while in the White House, so he only had a few substantive accomplishments. He failed to win a second term, but was later elected as a Massachusetts Representative.

Adams kept a diary during his time in public office, which reveals a very strong faith. Adams could not accept Christianity without miracles, and he believed that if you accept one miracle in the Bible, you have to accept them all. He was very outspoken about his relationship with Jesus as his Savior and Redeemer. He once said, "The hope of a Christian is inseparable from his faith. Whoever believes in the divine inspiration of the Holy Scriptures must hope that the religion of Jesus shall prevail throughout the earth."

Paul the Apostle (ca. 5 – 67)

For you will be His witness to all men of what you have seen and heard.
Acts 22:15

Paul the Apostle was a great missionary evangelist, but he wasn't always faithful to Christ. He started out as a persecutor of Christians. He later had a life-changing meeting with Jesus, which changed his heart. He became champion and hero to Christians.

Paul was born as Saul of Tarsus around A.D. 5. He was of Benjamite lineage and Hebrew ancestry. His parents were Pharisees and adhered strictly to the Law of Moses. He was sent to Palestine in his teens to study under a rabbi named Gamaliel. Saul mastered Jewish history, the Psalms, and the works of the prophets. He went on to become a lawyer.

Saul was determined to eradicate Christians. He was ruthless in his pursuit because he believed he was doing the work of God. According to Acts 8:3, he entered homes, dragged men and women off to prison; he was a religious terrorist.

One day, on the road to Damascus, a 150 mile-journey, Saul met Jesus Christ. Saul had been on a murderous rampage against Christians prior to this meeting and he was on his way to persecute Christians. On the road, Saul was faced with a bright light from heaven that caused him to fall face first to the ground. Jesus spoke to him, asking why he was persecuting him. This was the turning point in Saul's life.

Saul submitted to the Lord and wanted to know what he could do to. He wanted to show his obedience through works. Instead, Jesus told him that salvation does not come from works. Although he was blinded from the bright light, Saul obeyed Jesus' order to go into the city. It was there that Saul prayed to receive the Holy Spirit and was baptized. Saul began proclaiming Jesus as the Son of God. Saul became known as Paul after his transformation. People were reluctant to trust Paul because of his reputation as a persecutor of Christians. With the help of other believers, Paul succeeded in spreading the news of the Savior.

He wrote many of the New Testament books, including Romans, 1 Corinthians, 2 Corinthians, Galatians, Philippians, 1 Thessalonians, 2 Thessalonians, Philemon, Ephesians, Colossians, 1 Timothy, 2 Timothy, and Titus.

Paul spent his life, after the transformation, proclaiming the risen Christ. He traveled the Roman world, often in great peril. He died a martyr's death in prison in the 60s A.D. Paul's life story is found in the Book of Acts in the New Testament of the Bible.

Martin Luther King Jr. (1929 – 1968)

If we say that we have fellowship with Him, and walk in darkness, we lie and do not practice truth. But if we walk in the light as He is in the light, we have fellowship with one another, and the blood of Jesus Christ His Son cleanses us from all sin. 1 John 1:6-7

Martin Luther King Jr. was a social advocate and Baptist Minister. He led the Civil Rights Movement in the United States. He, along with many other civil rights leaders of the time, founded the Southern Christian Leadership Conference (SCLC).

He was born Michael King Jr. in Atlanta, Georgia in 1929. His father and grandfather were both Baptist preachers, he would soon follow in their footsteps, including the choice to change his name in honor of the great Protestant leader, Martin Luther. He was publically educated from the age of 5 and attended Morehouse College in Atlanta at 15 years old. He received a sociology degree in 1948 and went on to Crozer Theological Seminary in Pennsylvania. He received his doctorate from Boston University.

He led the Civil Rights Movement of the 1950s and 1960s. He had a huge impact on race relations and helped to end segregation of African-Americans. In 1963, he gave his famous "I Have a Dream" speech. It was a powerful and influential catapult for race relations in America. "I have a dream that my four children will one day live in a nation where they will not be judged by the color of their skin but by the content of their character." –Martin Luther King, Jr.

He played an important role in the creation of the Civil Rights Act of 1964, which outlawed discrimination based on race, religion, sex, or national origin. It ended racial segregation in schools, the workplace, and other public facilities. He also played a pivotal role in the creation of the Voting Rights Act of 1965, a law that prohibits racial discrimination in voting.

King received the Nobel Peace Prize in 1964. He was assassinated in 1968 and is remembered as one of the most important African-American leaders in history.

John Wesley (1703 – 1791)

Hold fast the pattern of sound words which you have heard from me, in faith and love which are in Christ Jesus. 2 Timothy 1:13

John Wesley was a minister in the Church of England who co-founded Methodism. He was known for his incredible work ethic and diligence, especially when it came to spreading the Gospel.

Wesley was born in Epworth, England in 1703. He was one of nineteen children. His father was an Anglican priest and his mother home-schooled the children. His mother had a profound influence on Wesley. His home life was rigid and structured, which is where Wesley learned to be obedient and hardworking. He attended Oxford and was a gifted scholar. He was eventually ordained unto the Anglican ministry.

In 1738, Wesley attended a religious meeting in London. According to his journal, at this meeting, after many years of being frustrated with his ministry, he realized that he could only touch other people's hearts if his heart was touched by Christ.

After this meeting, Wesley wrote the following in his journal:

"In the evening, I went very unwillingly to a society in Aldersgate Street, where one was reading Luther's preface to the Epistle to the Romans. About a quarter before nine, while he was describing the change which God works in the heart through faith in Christ, I felt my heart strangely warmed. I felt I did trust in Christ, Christ alone for salvation, and an assurance was given me that he had taken away my sins, even mine, and saved me from the law of sin and death."

This "heartwarming" is considered the beginning of the Methodist movement. He did not want to leave the Church of England; however, circumstances and his diligence led to the newfound denomination. He then began to take his ministry to the working class, the fields and factories, where his message was accepted enthusiastically. The Methodist movement grew rapidly, from meetings in homes to larger classes.

Wesley travelled more than 4000 miles per year, mostly on horseback, and preached tens of thousands of sermons over his lifetime. Wesley was a well-loved and respected man of God. He was still preaching when he died at 88 years old. As a result of his organizational genius, we know exactly how many followers he had when he died - 294 preachers, 71,668 British members, 19 missionaries, 198 American preachers, and 43,265 American members. Today, there are over 30 million Methodists worldwide.

Nicolaus Copernicus (1473 – 1543)

Lift up your eyes on high, and see who has created these things, Who brings out their host by number; He calls them all by name, By the greatness of His might and the strength of His power; not one is missing. Isaiah 40:26

Nicolaus Copernicus was a Polish astronomer who identified the concept of a heliocentric solar system, in which the sun is the center of the solar system. He was a master of all things mathematics, astronomy, medicine, and theology. He revolutionized how people thought of their world and their God.

Copernicus was born in 1473 in Torun, Poland. His parents were wealthy, his dad a prominent businessman. He was very well educated and strong in his faith. He was a Canon in the Catholic Church. He studied painting and mathematics at the University of Cracow and later received his doctorate of law at the University of Padua. While he did study astronomy, his focus in school was on law and medicine; astronomy was more of hobby for him. After meeting Domenico Maria Novara, a famous astronomer, he became fascinated with astronomy.

He spent his life out of the limelight. He was not one to make bold, public statements; even hesitating to publish his revolutionary views until just before his death. Copernicus considered it his "loving duty to seek the truth in all things, in so far as God has granted that to human reason." It was this passion for truth that gave Copernicus the drive to seek the truth despite the consequences he may face.

At the end of his life, Copernicus published a book stating that the earth and planets revolve around the sun. This is in contrast to the old belief that the planets and sun revolve around the earth. His ideas were too much for the church at this time. In 1616, the church made it illegal to teach Copernicus' theory as fact.

Later, when Galileo came along, he saw Copernicus' ideas as revolutionary in how humankind conceived of itself. His ideas were instrumental in the advancement of the field of astronomy. All who preceded him were influenced by his theories.

John Wycliffe (ca. 1330 – 1384)

And do not be conformed to this world, but be transformed by the renewing of your mind, that you may prove what is good and acceptable and perfect will of God. Romans 2:12

John Wycliffe was an English philosopher, theologian, lay preacher, teacher, and church reformer. He was in the midst of most of the religious and political controversies of his day.

John Wycliffe was born into a large family in 1330 in the village of Hipswell in the North Riding of Yorkshire. He studied at Oxford in the 1340s, and then stayed very well connected to the school for the remainder of his life.

Surrounded by greed and immorality amongst the leaders of the church, Wycliffe took his responsibilities as a pastor very seriously. He knew the church needed moral reform and he spoke out against the immorality and superstitious cult of relics within the church. He wrote about his conflicts with the church. He questioned the doctrine of transubstantiation. He questioned the position of the pope and challenged the indulgences of the pope's lifestyle. He also repudiated the confessional saying, "Private confession…was not ordered by Christ and was not used by the apostles."

Wycliffe led a rebellious movement in the 14th century. His followers were called Lollards; they preached anticlerical reforms and acted as the precursor to the Protestant Reformation of the 16th and 17th centuries. He is known as the Morning Star of the Reformation. They were eventually forced underground, but they persisted in their cause.

Wycliffe was one of the earlier advocates of translating the Bible. He believed that every Christian should have access to the Word of God; however, the church did not agree. The Bible was only available in Latin translations at the time, so he began to translate the Bible in English with the help of his followers. He got into trouble when he translated the Bible into English. The church claimed, "...the Scriptures have become vulgar...So the pearl of the gospel is scattered and trodden underfoot by swine." His writings were banned by a church council, but they eventually made the way into the hands of Christians.

Wycliffe left a powerful impression on the church. Despite the suppression of his teachings, they continued to spread long after his death in 1384. Although, his body was eventually dug up and burned because the Council of Constance considered him a "heretic", most people regarded him as a saint.

Mother Teresa (1910 – 1997)

This is My commandment, that you love one another as I have loved you. Greater love has no one than this, than to lay down one's life for his friends. John 15: 12-13

Mother Teresa was a Roman Catholic sister and missionary to the hungry, poor, helpless, and forgotten people. She founded the Order of Missionaries of Charity.

Agnes Gonxha Bojaxhiu was born of Albanian heritage in Skopje, Macedonia in 1910. She was fascinated by stories of the lives of missionaries and at age twelve she was convinced she would commit herself missions. She left home at 18 years old to join the Sisters of Loreto. She eventually began a citizen of India and lived most of her life there.

Mother Teresa was the founder of the Missionaries of Charity, it is a Roman Catholic congregation that runs hospices and homes, Centers for people with disabilities, soup kitchens, dispensaries, and mobile clinics, family counseling services, orphanages, and schools. Today, Missionaries for Charity is active in 133 countries. The over 4500 Catholic sisters have to adhere to a vow of chastity, poverty, and obedience in order to be members. They are also required to give "wholeheartedly free service to the poorest of the poor."

Mother Teresa dedicated her life to missions and giving of herself. She received many awards for her kindness and selflessness, including the Nobel Peace Prize for her work as a humanitarian in 1979. She has been memorialized through museums and a variety of other structures. She is loved by many for her charitable works and giving heart. Her life is a true example of selfless giving. Even after her death, we can all learn from her example, "Let us not be satisfied with just giving money. Money is not enough, money can be got, but they need your hearts to love them. So, spread your love everywhere you go."

Jonathan Edwards (1703 – 1758)

Therefore the Lord said: Inasmuch as these people draw near with their mouths and honor me with their lips, but have removed their hearts far from Me, and their fear toward Me is taught by the commandment of men.
Isaiah 29:13

Jonathan Edwards was a Christian preacher, philosopher, and theologian. He is known as one of the great preachers in colonial America. Edwards dedicated his life to the service of God. His followers were known as the New Light Calvinist ministers.

Edwards was born in East Windsor, Connecticut in 1703. He was the son of a Puritan pastor, the only boy out of eleven children. He was fascinated with science and theology. He entered Yale at twelve years old. He studied divinity and graduated as Valedictorian four years later. He received his Masters degree in three years. Edward's was ordained minister at Northampton.

As a preacher, Edward's sermons were very passionate and are considered treasured pieces of American Puritan literature. His sermons were a part of the revival known as the Great Awakening. He wrote a book entitled *Faithful Narrative of the Surprising Work of God.* It was all about the Great Awakening. He insisted that "true religion, in great parts, consists in holy affections." He believed that a man has to be emotionally engaged with God; otherwise, nothing mattered.

Edwards was fascinated by Isaac Newton's scientific discoveries. Before he became a full-time preacher, he wrote about topics in natural philosophy. He saw the laws of nature as God's way showing His wisdom and care.

Although he is remembered for his famous hellfire sermon called, "Sinners in the Hands of an Angry God," Edwards preached about God's love more than His wrath. His life was characterized by his intellect and piety. He was truly one of the great men of American history. His writings continue to influence people even today.

Michelangelo (1475 – 1564)

Therefore I remind you to stir up the gift of God which is in you through the laying on of My hands. 2 Timothy 1:6

Michelangelo di Lodovico Buonarroti is possibly the greatest Christian sculptor of all time and one of the greatest painters as well. He was also an architect and poet, writing over 300 sonnets and madrigals.

Michelangelo was born in 1475 in Caprese, Italy. He grew up near a marble quarry and joked that he absorbed marble dust as a kid. He did not receive much formal education, but became an apprentice in Florence at a young age. His work was highly sought after by the pope and he was commissioned on many occasions by the Pope.

He began sculpting when he was very young. He produced many biblical figures over the years. *Pieta* was his first masterpiece, showing Christ dead in his mother's arms. *David* was his most famous piece and one of the most famous statues in the world, standing almost fourteen feet tall. Another notable sculpture was *Moses,* showing him holding the Ten Commandments.

He was not only a world-famous sculptor, but also a very talented painter. He was commissioned by Pope Julius II to paint the ceiling of the Sistine Chapel. He covered the ceiling with beautiful figures from the Bible, including the famous image of David reaching out to God. It took him years to complete, most of which he spent lying on his back.

His final masterpiece was painted on a 48 by 44 foot wall. It was called *The Last Judgment.* It portrayed the saints as they entered heaven and the damned as they entered into hell.

Michelangelo was very fascinated by the human face and body, as well as God. Many of the artists of his time were immoral and their work represented their worldly beliefs; however, Michelangelo was a devout Catholic and his work represented that. Also known as, "the father and master of all arts," he is considered the greatest artist of all time and his work still influences people around the world today.

Ludwig van Beethoven (1770 – 1827)

I will praise the name of God with a song, and it will magnify him with thanksgiving. Psalm 69:30

Ludwig van Beethoven was a German composer and pianist. He played an important role in the transition period between the Classical to Romantic eras of music. He is one of the most famous and influential composers of all time.

Beethoven was born in Bonn, Germany. He was very talented from an early age. His first recital was held when Beethoven was just seven years old. Beethoven's father pushed him at a very early age. He was forced to practice and was beat for mistakes or hesitation, his father trained him harshly in hopes that he would become as the great Mozart. He was not a good student; some believed he was mildly dyslexic. He said himself that "Music comes to me more readily than words." At ten years old, he left school to study music full time.

Beethoven published his first composition at twelve years old. In 1787, he went to Vienna to study with Mozart. At that time, Mozart said of Beethoven's audition, "Keep your eyes on him; some day he will give the world something to talk about." Beethoven was an innovator when it came to music composition, combining voice and instruments in a new way. He composed many works over the years, including his best known works, 9 symphonies, 5 concertos for piano, 1 opera, 2 masses, 32 piano sonatas, and many more.

Over time, Beethoven began to lose his hearing. He tried his best to conceal it, but his hearing was worsening quickly. However, Beethoven continued to compose music and did so brilliantly after he was completely deaf.

Beethoven was not an active churchgoer, but he did have a firm belief in an ultimate, benign, and intelligent Power. He also showed an interest in "church music" and often studied the composers.

Tertullian (160 – 225)

Go therefore and make disciples of all the nations, baptizing them in the name of the Father and of the Son and of the Holy Spirit. Matthew 28:19

Tertullian was an important Christian author, apologist, polemicist, and theologist. He was instrumental in shaping the vocabulary and thought of Western Christianity. He is known as "the founder of Western theology.

Quintus Septimius Florens Tertullianus was born in Carthage. Not much is known about his life. Most of what we know was pieced together from his writing. He was born to pagan parents and it is thought that his father was a centurion. He received a well-rounded education and excelled in language, philosophy, and law. He later moved to Rome to further his education. He became a lawyer, and some believe, an ordained priest.

While in Rome, he became interested in the Christian movement; however, it wasn't until he later returned to Carthage that he was converted to Christianity. Tertullian was a talented teacher and apologist and emerged as a leading member of the North African Church.

Tertullian devoted his life to literacy pursuits. He was the first Christian author to produce an extensive corpus of Latin Christian literature. He was eloquent in both Greek and Latin. He spent much of his time defending his Catholic faith to the pagans. He coined some of the key terms and phrases of the Christian theological tradition, such as the term *Trinitas, or Trinity* to describe the Father, Son, and Holy Spirit, "one God in three persons." He also coined other Catholic doctrines, such as Christology, ecclesiology, and sacramental theology.

He was the author of more than thirty apologetic and theological works, as well as one of the most quoted of the Early Church Fathers. He challenged the pagan religions of the Roman Empire, as well as the heretical versions of Christianity. He set out to argue the case for

Christianity and correct the misconceptions about the faith. His writings certainly made an impression on the pagan world. He also played a role in boosting the church's self-confidence.

Ulrich Zwingli (1484 – 1531)

You are my hiding place and my shield; I hope in your word. Psalm 119:114

Ulrich Zwingli was a Roman Catholic priest and a leader of the Protestant Reformation in Switzerland.

Zwingli was born into a large farming family was born in 1484 in the Toggenburg valley of Switzerland. He studies music and philosophy at the University of Vienna and the University of Basel where he received his Master of Arts degree.

Zwingli was the Zurich city chaplain and was very outspoken about his ideas on reforming the Catholic Church. He did not follow any particular theological model; he seemed to have his own unique model of theology that was revealed over time through his sermons. He opposed clerical celibacy, marrying a widow who had three children. He opposed fasting during lent; so much so, that he and his followers ate sausages in public to break the fast. He was also strongly against Catholic pardons (pardons that were meant to free a person's soul from purgatory). He attacked the church's use of images in places of worship and he eventually abolished the mass in Zurich and replaced it with a more simple service.

Zwingli was a contemporary of Martin Luther who does not get enough credit for his role in the Protestant Reformation. He actually fought for change before Luther. Like Luther, he believed that the Bible should be given priority over church laws and he also opposed the sale of indulgences because he saw officials abusing them by selling them to raise money for the church. He condemned this doctrine in Switzerland long before Luther's *95 Thesis*. Luther and Zwingli agreed on many of the church doctrines, such as the Trinity, for example; however, they could not agree on the presence of Jesus in the Eucharist, so he broke ties with Luther.

Zwingli was a humanist and scholar that had many devoted followers. He was killed in battle at Kappel while defending Zurich against an attack by the Catholic cantons of southern Switzerland. Unlike some of the reformers of his time, his movement did not evolve into a church; but his legacy lives on in the Reformed churches of today.

William Penn (1644 – 1718)

For the body is one and has many members, but all the members of that one body, being many, are on body, so also is Christ. 1 Corinthians 12:12

William Penn was an English Quaker who founded the Province of Pennsylvania. He was a leader and advocate of religious freedom.

William Penn was born into a distinguished Anglican family in London, England in 1644. He was educated at Chigwell School in Essex. He also attended Christ Church College, but was expelled for his criticism of the Church. He then studied theology at the Protestant Academy in France. He returned to England, where he studied law.

He rebelled against the Church of England and he converted to the religious group known as the Society of Friends, also known as Quaker religion in his twenties. He became a devout Quaker and advocate for the doctrines. Penn's father did not approve of his religious views. He began to fight for freedom for his religious group, and was jailed many times for his resistance to the Church.

King Charles II owed Penn's father a great deal of money; and to pay off that debt, the king granted Penn the right to establish a new colony in America. He received a charter for territory in 1681 from King Charles II. He became the governor of this new colony that the king named Pennsylvania. His intentions were to have a place where there was no established church and therefore, no persecution or harassment.

This new colony had immediate success because it drew many Quakers, as well as others looking for religious freedom. Penn's colony was different. All people were welcomed into Pennsylvania, regardless of their religious views. He insisted that the Indians be treated with honor and respect. In fact, a treaty was signed that said that the Indians and colonists would "live in love as long as the sun gave light." He set forth democratic principles that later served as inspiration for the United States Constitution. The colony was a success

In 1984, Ronald Reagan issued an Act of Congress by Presidential Proclamation 5283 that declared Penn an Honorary United States Citizen. There is a statue of Penn on top of City Hall in Philadelphia Pennsylvania.